HINDUISM IN MANIPUR

HINDUISM IN MANIPUR

In the Eighteenth and Nineteenth Centuries and its Impact on Contemporary Society and Culture with Special Focus on Religious and Cultural Assimilation, Syncretization and Integration

G.P. Singh

GYAN

Hinduism in Manipur

ISBN: 978-81-212-1139-0

Published in 2012 in India by
Gyan Publishing House
23, Main Ansari Road
New Delhi-1100052
Phones : 23282060, 23261060
Fax : 011-23285914
E-mail: books@gyanbooks.com
Website: www.gyanbooks.com

Laser Typesetting : Quick Media, Delhi
Printed at : Chawla Offset Printers, Delhi

CONTENTS

PREFACE

This treatise deals with history of Hinduism in Manipur in the eighteenth and nineteenth centuries and its impact on the contemporary society and culture with focus on religious and cultural assimilation, syncretization and integration. It throws light on the impact of Hinduism on all aspects of life and culture of the Meitei people in the valley of Manipur.

The work is based on native chronicles, numismatic and epigraphic evidence and other reliable sources.

The work, I believe, will be useful to those who intend to carry out further historical disquisition into the subject.

G.P. Singh

1

HINDUISM IN MANIPUR

Scholars are divided in their opinion regarding the antiquity, variety and vitality of Hinduism in Manipur. It is really a difficult task to present the history of evolution of Hinduism in Manipur in a systematic manner and chronological order. We have but little information about the stages the history of Hinduism passed through in the centuries preceding the eighteenth. We, however, get a clear picture of the subject when we come to the eighteenth century which marked the opening of a new chapter in the history of Hinduism in Manipur. With that century Hinduism entered on a new phase. Substantial progress was made in the field of the growth of Hinduism during the eighteenth and nineteenth centuries about which we have a lot of valuable information. The striking difference between the earlier and later phases of religious beliefs and practices of the people in the valley of Manipur can be noticed. The difference is not wholly chronological but perceptional. The worship of the new deities grew up in the midst of the indigenous ones. The transition is obscured but also was facilitated by the emergence of new religious ideas and philosophy during the period.

II

Shaivism, Shaktism and Tantrism–the three important sects or forms of Hinduism–first deserve our notice. There wege different stages in the evolution of these three forms of Hinduism in Manipur. The prevalence of Shaiva, Shakti and Tantric cults in Manipur before and after the advent of Vaishnavism can be fairly attested to by traditional accounts, literary and archaeological data and other reliable evidence. We have a very interesting accounts of the emergence and growth of the aforesaid three popular religious cults which became gradually popular in Manipur. Some occasional developments, historical changes, socio-religious factors, etc. also conditioned the growth of Hinduism in its variant forms.

Shaivism has a long history. The worship of Shiva—one of the important deities of Hindu pantheon of Puranic fame—began in Manipur in very early times and further continued. The concept of Shaivism in Manipur was based on the philosophy of *Ekesvarvad* which marks the Rudra or Mahadeva of Vedic antiquity. The oldest form of

Hinduism–Shaivism–is marked by the worship of Shiva through the phallic form of lingam. The concept of Shaivism associated with phallus or lingam was known to the people in Manipur valley. The adoration of Shiva in the form of phallic emblem was very popular in Manipur. The worship of Shiva in the form of phallic symbol in Sanahal Lokchou hill area was prevalent till the beginning of the nineteenth century.

The Shaivism in Manipur was also associated with the fertility cult. The women-folk are believed to have paid their homage to Shiva–linga–the reproductive organ of Shiva–for their fertility and good progeny.

As a result of the growing influence of brahmanical religion and culture in Manipur between the fifteenth and nineteenth century, Shaivism received an impetus at the hands of brahmanas. The debased form of Shaivism was replaced by the purer form of Shaivism. During the period noted above, the Shaiva cult became popular to a considerable extent. The brahmanas also might have contributed to the growth of Shaivism in Manipur during the period.

The stone conch of Mahadeva or Shiva as referred to in the book *Shagok Shading* also provides evidence to the importance of Shaivism in Manipur during the time of king Charairongba (CE 1697-1709).

During the time of king Bhagyachandra (CE 1759-98), Shaivism received the royal patronage. The king was greatly influenced by the revelation made by God Aditya that He is the incarnation of Shiva. He had such realisation in his dream. He received the direction from Prabhu Aditya in his dream with regard to the making of wooden image of the god. Accordingly the king installed the image of Aditya at Lamangdong which was worshipped by the people as an incarnation of Shiva.

Shiva was worshipped in Manipur in different forms at different places. He was worshipped as Nong- pok Ningtho at Takhen, Charangpau, Shallungtpham, Thongam Mondum and other places. He was also worshipped as Mahadeva at Nogmaijing or Nongmaiching, Heibok, Ingourok, Thongam Mondum, Kwarok, etc.

In the beginning of the nineteenth century, several shrines or temples dedicated to Shiva were constructed in Manipur. Quite a good number of shrines dedicated to Shiva have been found in the hills of the Manipur valley. In the hills, Shiva was worshipped in various forms, particularly the carved stones which signify Shivalingas. The temples dedicated to Shiva have been found in different hill areas of Manipur notably, Mount, Koubru, Nongmaiching hill (Nilakantha giri), Ingourok hill, Thongam Mondum hill, Heibok hill and Chinga or Chingoi hill (also called Shiva Nagar). The most important sect of Shaivism in Manipur has been fixed at Nogmaiching hill because of the constant attachment of Lord Shiva to this place. Maharaja Chandrakirti (CE 1834-44) is credited with having constructed the shrine of Shiva on Nogmaiching hill. The royal chronicle of Manipur confirms the truth that particularly during the time of that king the Shaiva cult became very popular.[1] The worship of phallic symbol on hill tops undoubtedly bears witness to the Shiva worship in Manipur. On many a hill top there still remains Shivalingas which people on special occasions worship and pray to.

It is unworthy of acceptance that by the seventeenth century ancient Shaivite Hinduism in Manipur had completely acceded to Vaishnavism or the cult of Vishnu. The fact remains that Shaiva cult like two other cults–Shakti and Tantric–was prevalent in Manipur before and after the introduction of Vaishnava faith in early eighteenth century.

The archaeological discovery of an image of Shiva in human form sculptured in sandstone and seated on a bull or Nandi and depicted with linga portion (kept on display in Mutua Museum Imphal)[2] also testifies to the prevalence of Shiva worship in Manipur down to the nineteenth century.

The image of Mahadeva (Shiva) along with Ganesha and Kartikeya are also kept on display in the State Museum, Imphal.

One image of Shiva with five heads was found lying in the Mahabali forest in the past, but details thereof are lacking because that god was not installed in any temple. However, it can be presumed that the Pasupat concept of Mahadeva was known to the people to some extent. Even today the people of Manipur go to Mahabali temple complex to worship Mahadeva.

It is a fact to reckon with that god Shiva with girdle of snakes, a trident in the hand and wearing tiger's skin was also worshipped in Manipur. This is also an indication of the worship of Shiva in an human form.

The worship of Shiva with one face and two arms was very common in Manipur. The stone image of Shiva in yogic posture with folded hands generally kept as a "gate keeper" in most of the Vaishnava temples was also adored. This image was probably carved as a model of "Dhani Buddha" in the Buddhist tradition. From the paintings it appears that an image of Shiva in a sitting posture with hemp (Bhang) in the right hand and flanked by the bull, trisul (trident) and kamandala was also worshipped. The artistic representation of a scene of falling of the Ganga to earth from Shiva's head and that of penance of Bhagirath and an image of Shiva in some temples in Manipur, and worship of phallus (symbolizing Shivalinga) in temples also bear testimony to the belief of the people in Shaivism. The worship of Shiva in the form of earthen images, stone-pieces, etc. has also been witnessed.

The above description leaves no doubt in our mind about the worship of Shiva in various forms. But relatively the worship of Shiva in the form of phallic symbol was widely prevalent. The influence of phallicism is still discernible in Manipur.

Shiva has been generally worshipped according to the puranic Hindu rites. The Brahmans, and Maibas and Maibis (local priests and priestesses respectively) usually performed the priestly functions at the time of worshipping Shiva. Shiva is also believed to have been worshipped as a tutelary deity of the kings of Manipur. The worship of Shiva in the form of Nongpok Ningthou was conducted according to animistic rites.

The worship of Shiva and Durga became popular particularly through the festivals. The worship of the former on three auspicious days of the year–Sivaratri day, Varuni day and Chairouba day–is still very common. These three indigenous festivals, which were very popular in the eighteenth and nineteenth centuries, are still held here. The Varuni festival held in honour of Shiva is believed to have been imported into Manipur from Bengal. But, on the other hand, it is accepted as an indigenous festival the popularity of which is generally ascribed to the reign of Chandrakirti.

The mingling of different traditions of worshipping Shiva at different places at different periods of history, including the eighteenth and nineteenth centuries, gave a new turn to the concept of Shaivism.

The gradual decline of Shiva worship may precisely be attributed to its subordination to the Vaishnava cult. The adoption of Trantic practices by the worshippers of Shiva also led to the unpopularity of this cult to some extent. However, it must be admitted that in spite of the popularity of Vaishnava cult of Hinduism, Shaivism never lost its ground. The most prominent aspect of Shaivism in Manipur was the firm belief of the people in the worship of Shiva in the form of linga or phallic emblem. Shiva worship has, of course, declined but not totally disappeared in Manipur.

The remarkable religion known as Shaktism, which stands for the worship of Shakti under various names of which Devi, Durga and Kali are the best known, has its own place among the principal/sub-divisions of Hinduism. It regards the goddess as the active manifestation of the shakti or enegy. The impersonation of the female energy in the form of Mother goddess or the worship of the active female principle constitutes one of its important aspects. Both male and female principles have been recognized as dynamic aspects of Hinduism. In fact, the Shakti worship seems to be rather older than Shiva worship. Shaktism appears to be a compound of Hinduism with un-Aryan beliefs. It acquired great influence both in the courts and among the people of north-eastern India (especially Assam and Manipur) but without producing personalities of much eminence as teachers, preachers or writers.

The Shakti cult or Mother goddess cult like Shaiva cult became very popular in Manipur during the period under notice. Equal importance was given to both the male-gods (*lais*) and the female goddesses (*lai rembis*). The dual conception of Shaivism and Shaktism in Manipur constitutes one of the striking features of Hinduism that flourished here.

Lairembi or Mother goddess assumed different names in Manipur. She was worshipped under various local names such as Nongpok-Panthoibi, Irai-Leima, Soubon-Lairema, Leinao-Tabi, Phaoibi, Leimarel, Yumjao-Leirembi, Konthoujam-Lairembi, Soubon-Lairembi, and Heishnam-Lairembi. The female deities of the Meitei pantheon as enumerated above are also the manifestations of Shakti worship in local tradition. Their worship went on side by side with the female deities of the Hindu pantheon which constitutes one of the glaring illustrations of religious syncretism.

During the time of king Charairongba, the goddess Kali was worshipped by a large section of Meitei population. This is proved by the construction of two Kali temples during his time, one in 1706 and other in 1707.[3] The native chronicle records the contruction of another temple dedicated to goddess Kali. But unfortunately it was burnt along with other buildings in an accidental fire. Further, from the chronicle it also appears that a separate temple for Panthoibi ((Devi) was constructed and her image was also moulded.[4] The account given in the chronicle has been strongly supported by J. Shakespear[5], one of the authorities on the religion of Manipur. The epigraphic evidence[6] also confirms the worship of goddess during the time of said king. The popularity of Shakti cult in early part of the eighteenth century can incontrovertibly be proved by the available evidences. When the Hinduisation process started in the valley of Manipur in the early part of that century when king Charairongba was reigning, Panthoibi–the supreme among the female goddesses of the Meitei pantheon–was identified with goddess Kali of the Hindu pantheo. Later, she was identified more with goddess Durga than Kali. The worship of indigenous goddesses together with Hindu goddesses during the eighteenth and following centuries goes to show the faith of the people in the cult of Shakti.

"...the material available to us," says S.N. Parrott, "does not permit us to conclude that Saivism and Durga worship are any older than Vaishnavism in Manipur...Durga worship was introduced late in the reign of Charairongba...Siva worship entered at a rather later date."[7] As already stated, Shaivism or Shiva worship was prevalent in Manipur both before and after the advent of Vaishnavism. Durga worship was, of course introduced for the first time during the reign of Charairongba. Durga and Kali–the two powerful representatives of Shakti–were worshipped in conformity with the Hindu tradition.

The period (CE 1709-48) of Gopal Singh generally called Garib Niwaz was very eventful from the point of view of worship of Hindu goddesses Kali and Durga and other goddesses. From the native chronicle it appears that panthoibi was worshipped by Brahmans during his time. The goddess was earlier worshipped by Maibas and Maibis or the local priests and priestesses.[8] The chronicle also refers to the temple of Kalika (a Devi) built at Ningthem Pukhri. The members of Sairem family inhabiting this area used to worship the goddess in the temple.[9] In 1725, the stone image of Khutleima (Devi) was shifted from Kangla to Ninghtem Pukhri on the occasion of a particular ceremony. The chronicle also bears witness to the fact that in 1726 a stone image of Kali was set up[10] which was later recovered from a large tank (Ningthem Pukhri) in the course of its draining in 1906.[11] The discovery of this image also points to the popularity of Skakti cult in the early eighteenth century. It may further be added here that a temple was dedicated to Durga by king Garib Niwaz at Heibok hill at the instance of Shantidasa who came from Sylhet to Manipur during his time. The popular tradition affirms it that two Gosain (including Shantidasa) came from Sylhet not only to popularize Ramandi cult of Vaishnavism but also the Shakti cult of Hinduism in Manipur. As a matter of fact, both the Shakti and Vaishnava cults of Hinduism flourished in Manipur during the time of the said king.

King Bhagyachandra had equal respect for all sects of Hinduism, including Shaiva, Shakti and Vaishnava and indigenous religion because of his catholicity of outlook and broad mindedness. During the time of that great king, some of the traditional gods and goddesses were identified with Hindu gods and goddesses as a result of the complete Hinduisation in Manipur valley. As for instance, Nongpok Ningthou of Koubru became God Shiva and Lairembi (Devi) of Hiyangthang Goddess Kamakhya. The king himself used to worship Devi.

The importance of the sacred place known as Hiyangthang (Kamakhya of Manipur) as one of the Sakta-pithas and its association with the worship of Durga need to be highlighted here. In fact, it is one of the Sakta-pithas of India. The famous Tantra literature[12] also includes Manipur in the list of forty-two Sakta-pithas of India. In fact, there are 51 Sakta-pithas in India. It is traditionally believed that wherever the organs of Sati fell that turned into Sakta-pithas. She was daughter of Daksha Prajapati and her dead body was cut into 51 pieces by Vishnu. The waist of Sati, according to the said Tantra literature, fell at Hiyangthang and the temple at this place which is still in existence is believed to have enshrined the relic. Since then Manipur came to be known as Mekhali Desha. "...a temple of considerable fame", observes T.C. Hodson. "for here abides the Hindu goddess Durga, who is known to have avenged an insult to her shrine by causing the death of the sacrilegious. In this temple there is a black stone...This was the Laipham of the dread goddess."[13] Actually, it is not the images but the pieces of the plantain logs covered with phanek (dress of female) representing the waist of the deity which are worshipped in the temple. The antiquity of this Sakta-pitha has often been debated among the native scholars. No definite date can be suggested about its ancientness. However, the worship of Devi Kamakhya in the form of Shakti in the temple at Hiyanthang on a large scale in the latter half of the eighteenth century cannot be denied.

Durga worship no doubt shot into prominence during the reign of Bhagyachandra. From the available evidence[14] it is quite clear that the celebration of Durga Puja on a large scale began for the first time during his reign. Hiyangthang has been one of the famous seats of Durga worship in Manipur from his time. This place like the shrine of Heibok Mahadeva is a sacred one for all the Hindus, and Durga Puja is still celebrated here.

King Chourjit (CE 1803-13) is believed to have performed a yajna or sacrifice at Hiyangthang to put down the rebellion of his brother Madhuchandra, who was king of Manipur from CE 1801 to 1803. The former had firm belief in Shakti and Tantric cults of Hinduism.

According to an epigraphic evidence,[15] Maharaja Gambhir Singh (CE 1825-34) was also worshipper of Devi. He is believed to have constructed a temple for the goddess. The sacred place of Heishnam Lairemma (a goddess) located in the compound of First Manipur Rifle, Imphal, has been considered a place of worship.

The Shakti cult reached its zenith of progress by the time of Maharaja Chandrakirti (CE 1834-44). By that time Durga worship became widely prevalent and the traditional mother goddess cult became popular. On the authority of the royal chronicle of Manipur it can be asserted that Hiyangthang's Lairembi (Devi) became known as Kamakhya much before 1843.[16]

The identification of the great goddess in the Meitei pantheon called Panthoibi with Durga was one of the remarkable features of the religious history of medieval Manipur. Panthoibi has always been worshipped as the presiding deity in Manipur. The practice of worshipping this goddess became very helpful in the development of Shaktism in the local tradition of the Meiteis. Likewise, the worship of goddesses/Durga and Kali gave fillip to the development of Shaktism as one of the popular sects of Hinduism in the Hindu tradition.

The popularity of the Shakti cult can also be proved by the fact that from the time of Garib Niwaz onwards Kali was worshipped by the potentates and the populace in the shrine dedicated to the goddess.

The celebration of Durga Puja festival in Manipur, as described by T.C. Hodson[17], J. Johnstone[18] and E. W. Dun[19] and as narrated in the chronicle[20] also provides some clues about the worship of the mother goddess. In all likelihood,

Durga worship in its present form became very popular in Manipur during the times of Kings Garib Niwaz and Chandrakirti. In some of the shrines dedicated to the worship of Devi, the system of sacrifices was also in vogue. It is also to be noted that the worship of goddcss Kali representing the malevolent aspect of Devi is still popular in Manipur.

It is worthwhile to note that the worship of Devi by the kings and princes before launching an expedition against the hostile forces became a practice that was religiously followed in the eighteenth and nineteenth centuries. Further, it is to be added that Tantrism and the Vajrayana cult of Buddhism also influenced the evolution of Shaktism in Manipur.

It is very difficult to ascertain the exact period which marked the emergence of Tantrism as an offshoot of Hinduism. However, there are several indications which go to prove the existence of Tantric cult in Manipur. Here at the very outset, it can be mentioned that degenerated form of Buddhism that emerged in the early period and the brahmanical culture that spead in Manipur in the fifteenth century went a long way in the evolution of Tantric cult. Actually, the Tantrism that flourished in Manipur was nothing but a queer mixture of black magic, witchcraft, divination, shakti worship, etc. Tantrism in a broader sense is a system of magical or sacramental ritual which professes to attain the highest aim of religion by such methods as spells, diagrams and other exercises. It can be asserted with great amount of confidence that the Tantric cult of Hinduism had taken its root in the soil of Manipur in the early period itself like that in Assam. But before the dawn of fifteenth century it had not appeared on the scene in the magnified form. In the early period, it was greatly associated with the fertility cult, magical rites and rituals, etc. The incorporation of diverse cults and beliefs in the Meitei pantheon made the prospect of Tantrism very bright. The desire of the people to have some material and spiritual gain with the help of tantra, mantra, spells, prayers, magic, etc also furnished the pretext for the growth of this cult. It is also believed that the Tantric culture of Assam and Bengal had left some impact on Manipur in early period. The settlements of some wandering yogis or ascetics, well acquainted with the Tantric act, in Manipur at different periods of history are said to have afforded an opportunity for the common people to know about this art. The popular traditions and beliefs also help us throw light on the rise and growth of Tantric cult in Manipur.

The eighteenth century proved to be a fruitful period from the standpoint of the popularity of Tantric cult in Manipur. During the time of Garib Niwaz, a local pandit named Khongnangthaba entered into a dispute with Shantidasa (a religious preacher from Sylhet, as noted before) on the interpretations of the Tantric mantras. This proves that the local pandit had some idea about Tantrism. Tantrism could not stand in competition with Vaishnavism. Because the Vaishnava form of Hinduism acquired more popularity than Tantric form of Hinduism during the time of the said king. However, the faith of the people in the Tantric cult somehow helped it to survive. During the time of king Bhagyachandra, the people were following the Tantric practices. The importance of this cult had not completely declined because we find that the followers of this cult also existed during his time. But some of them who could not follow the Tantric practices sincerely and properly were punished by the king.

We have every reason to believe that in post-Garib Niwaz times Tantrism could not flourish much because the kings were vaishnavite by faith.

It failed to enjoy the royal patronage. However, there were some factors which kept the Tantric cult alive.

The Tantric mantras locally known as *Laiwas* (also called Jadu mantras), yantras (on which sometimes symbolic diagramme of the deity were inscribed), mudras or postures, yoga, and magical practices followed by the Maibas or priests, and pandits, became helpful in the evolution of Tantric cult in Manipur. The people of Manipur used the mantras for warding off all sorts of evil spirit. The people by and large had faith in the mantras or *laiwas*. The local pandits and the Maibas had thorough knowledge of the importance of the mantras. They also had faith in the Jadu-mantras. It was their firm belief that every spheres of life could be controlled by mantras. Here it must be made clear that the Tantric practices were followed by the people both in pre and post-Vaishnava period.

The destruction of Tantra literature by Shantidasa Gosain during the reign of Garib Niwaz in the wake of popularization of Vaishnava cult of Hinduism caused a great set back to the Tantric cult. However, it continued to survive.

Some Sanskrit words were used in the Tantric

mantras and hymns. The use of the symbol of *"OM"* and the words *Ka, Ma, Kling, Dring,* etc. proves that the local Pandits and priests were greatly inspired by Tantric mantras or *laiwas* and Tantric philosophy. Some of the Tantric words associated with Tantric practices were chanted on certain occasions which include socio-religious ceremonies and festivals.

The gradual development of the science of occultism, Tantric mantras, Jadu mantras, etc had great impact on the Tantric belief of the people. The introduction of barbaric Tantric rituals associated with human sacrifices in pre-Garib Niwaz times led to the debasement of Tantric practices of which we do not have any account at our disposal. The burning of local puyas and other works, dealing with human sacrifices and other aspects of Tantrism, to ashes during the time of Garib Niwaz has created a great vacuum in our knowledge of the subject.

The Tantric culture also flourished in the form of the worship of *umanglais* (forest gods). The nature of rituals connected with invocation of *Lairembis* (Devis) was greatly modified by the Tantric culture. When *Lairembi* became identified with Devi, the concept of Mother goddess and her worship for fertility, prosperity, and protection against all evil forces further left behind some ideas to be imbibed by the followers of Tantric cult. The worship of *Lairembis* was greatly associated with Tantrism. They were also treated as Tantric goddesses.

Some actions performed by the yogic Tantrics in the eighteenth and nineteenth centuries for the purpose of getting strength against all kinds of odds also furnish evidence of the prevalence of Tantric faith.

The performance of magical rites, and the Tantric pujas under the influence of Tantrics also had some impact on the Tantric faith of the people. It is traditionally believed that Shyam Sai, the eldest son of king Garib Niwaz, performed some magical rites for a number of days in the river. Such kind of practices were there even during the time of Bhagyachandra.

The reign of Chourjit proved to be a significant landmark in the history of Tantrism in Manipur. During his period, which is marked by the war of succession, the rival princes started performing Tantric practices with the help of Tantra, mantra, yoga, etc in order to get success in the contest for occupying the throne. They had blind faith in the

Tantric cult. In order to seek the blessings of the Mother goddesses and to get strength for facing any kind of political situation, they largely depended on Tantric practices. Thus, his period indirectly proved to be a boon for the growth of Tantric cult of Hinduism in Manipur.

On the basis of the analysis of the data available to us we can conclusively prove that Shaivism, Shaktism and Tantrism, which emerged as popular religious cults, greatly contributed to the rise and growth of Hinduism in Manipur. But these three cults of Hinduism could not become very popular because of the influence of the Vaishnava cult of Hinduism as well as the traditional Sanamahi cult on the religious beliefs and practices of the common people. Actually, all other sects of Hinduism were over shadowed by Vaishnavism which secured a firm ground in the eighteenth century. However, it cannot be denied that these three sects of Hinduism coexisted side by side with Vaishnavism and indigenous religion in Manipur during the period under notice. It will not be incorrect to say that Shaivism, Shaktism and Tantrism did not completely decline rather they survive more or less to this day.

There were various stages in the growth of Vaishnavism in Manipur. Vaishnava cult of Hinduism flourished during the period extending from the latter half of the fifteenth century to the early part of the nineteenth century. The antiquity of Vaishnavism in both regional and Indian contexts has been much debated by scholars. It was the reign of Kiyamba also called Kayamba (CE 1467-1508) which marked the advent of Vaishnavism in Manipur. There is no denying the fact that the Vishnu image was worshipped in Manipur as the family god of the ruling prince much before 1467, but the regular worship of Vishnu began from his time onwards. With the worship of Krishna as an incarnation of Vishnu in early eighteenth century the history of Vaishnavism took a new turn. The history of Vaishnava Hinduism in Manipur has been provided in detail in subsequent pages. Hinduism, the most popular and flourishing religion in Manipur in the eighteenth and nineteenth centuries, left an indelible impact on contemporary society and culture. In the treatment of the subject, the cultural assimilation and syncretization in Manipur and its religious, cultural and emotional integration with mainland India are also worthy of our notice.

III

The year 1704 constituted a landmark in the history of Hinduism in Manipur. Charairongba (CE 1697-1709) was the first Manipuri king to be formally initiated to Vaishnavism in that year. The royal chronicle of Manipur records that in Saka 1626 = CE 1704, on Wednesday, the fifth of Sajibu (April), a brahmana priest named Krishnacharya *alias* Rai Vanamali, who arrived in Manipur (in October 1703) from Shweta-Ganga, Puri (Orissa), initiated the king to Vaishnavism.[21] This marked the transition from Vishnushwami sect (famous for the worship of Vishnu) to Madhavacharya sect of Vaishnavism which stood for the worship of the image of Radha and Krishna. We are told by a native scholar that the image of Vishnu was kept as his family god.[22] After being converted to Hinduism in CE 1704, the king got his name changed to Pitambar Singh which is a clear-cut evidence of Sanskritization. His issued land grants to his brahmana guru for his settlement and maintenance. And he extended his patronage to Vaishnava sect of Hinduism which further flourished.

"With the accession of Charairongba we pass to the period in which Hinduism in one or other of its forms became the dominant religion of Manipur largely through the support and patronage of the reigning monarchs", observes S.N. Parratt.[23] She further asserts that "There is not very clear evidence of any Hinduising influence before the time of Charairongba."[24] She is absolutely correct in stating that "There is...no explicit reference to Hinduism in the years immediately before 1704 AD".[25]

T.C. Hodson (the chief authority on the history of the Meiteis) states that in Manipur "Hinduism was adopted as the state religion by royal edict (C. AD 1705)."[26] This statement is not recorded elsewhere. However, its trustworthiness cannot be doubted.

The school of Vaishnavism that the king Charairongba belonged to laid emphasis on the worship of Shri Krishna (an incarnation of Vishnu) as the supreme deity. In order to popularize the cult of Shri Krishna, he constructed a brick temple at Brahmapur Guru Aribam Leikai, Imphal, in CE 1707 and dedicated it to Shri Krishna.[27] This temple is still in excellent state of preservation. The image of Shri Krishna worshipped by the guru of the king is still adored by his descendants who are known as Guru-Aribam brahmanas. The said temple has been a place of worship for the Vaishnavites.

It is to be noted here that Charairongba was profoundly influenced by the philosophy that was preached by the followers of School of Nimbarka who flourished in the twelfth century (CE 1114-1162). He also followed Ramanuja (CE 1060-1137) whose exposition of qualified monism brought Vaishnavism to limelight. The worship of Radha and Krishna, the two important Hindu deities, became popular because of the impact of the basic doctrines of bhakti as emphasized by Nimbarka. It has been admitted by some authorities that Nimbarka's concept of bhakti in connection with the worship of Krishna and Radha greatly helped the growth of Vaishnavism.[28] With the spread of the knowledge of the Vaishnavite doctrines Hinduism started making progress during the time of the said king.

The popularity of Krishna cult during the time of king Charairongba can also be confirmed by a numismatic evidence. One inscribed bell-metal coin ascribed to the said king discovered at Heirok containing two lines on the obverse in Nagari script (i.e. Devanagari) refer to (1) *"Shri"* and (2) *"Krishna."*[29]

There is no doubt that it was Vaishnava form of Hinduism that was prevalent during the time of king Charairongba, but we cannot deny the popularity of the cult of Mother–goddess too during his time. In fact, some of the brahmanas of his time were not only the adherents of the Vaishnava faith but also the believers in the worship of the female deity-Kali. During his time, the goddess Kali was worshipped by a large section of the Meiteis. This is proved by the construction of several Kali temples during his time. The two famous Kali temples were built during his reign, one in CE 1706 and other in CE 1707, as we learn from the native chronicle. The chronicle records the construction of various temples including those of Kali during his reign. It further supplies us with the information that one of the two brick-built Kali temples suddenly collapsed only a few years after its construction because of the defects in workmanship. Some other Kali temples were burnt along with other buildings due to an accidental fire.[30]

During the reign of Charairongba, the worship of Panthoibi–the greatest goddess in the Meitei pantheon–continued along with that of Hindu deities like Vishnu, Durga and Kali. With the Hinduization of the king and acceptance of Hinduism as the religion, the identification of the local deities with the divinities of the Hindu pantheon began. The goddess Panthoibi was identified with Kali during his time. Later, its identification was preferred with Durga to Kali. That Hindu religion coexisted with indigenous one can be proved by the fact that the temples dedicated to both the indigenous and Hindu gods and goddesses were built almost simultaneously during his reign. Between CE 1707 and 1708 the temples for both Panthoibi and Kali were constructed, as recorded in the native chronicle.[31]

It is significant to note that king Charairongba did not make any serious attempt to establish Hinduism as a state religion nor did he neglect the worship of the traditional god (*lai*) and goddess (*lairembi*). The popular sanamahi cult too continued to hold its ground.

With the accession of Garib Niwaz (also called Pamheiba and Gopal Singh) in CE 1709 the history of Hinduism in Manipur took a different turn.

In Saka 1639 = CE 1717, in the month of Mera (October), Garib Niwaz, one of the renowned kings of Manipur, was formally initiated to Vaishnavism by his guru or preceptor Gopal Das, as recorded in the native chronicle.[32] It is said that first the potentate embraced the Vaishnava form of Hinduism and then the populace. It has also been observed that a large number of people were brought within the fold of Hinduism.[33] The declaration of

Vaishnava form of Hinduism as the state religion by the king[34] marked the opening of a new chapter in the religious history of medieval Manipur. The year 1717 witnessed a change from Madhavacharya sect of Vaishnavism to Chaitanya Vaishnavism. After having initiated the king and his followers to Chaitanya cult of Vaishnavism, guru Gopal Das returned to his native place three years later in CE 1720.

The king followed the Bengal School or Chaitanya School of Vaishnavism for twelve years (CE 1717-28). This school laid great emphasis on the worship of Shri Krishna as the supreme deity and that of his consort Radha. According to the doctrines expounded by the founders of this school, Shri Krishna was looked upon as the full incarnation of Vishnu and worshipped as the supreme God. This God was worshipped in accordance with the principles laid down in *Shrimad Bhagavata.*

As a result of the royal support extended to Chaitanya School of Vaishnavism, the worship of the gods and goddess of Vaishnava faith received wide popularity.

Chaitanya (CE 1485-1533), a contemporary of Vallabbacharya (CE 1479-1530), was a great Vaishnava preacher. He also came under the influence of Madhava sect (named after Madhavacharya, CE 1199-1278). He wanted to popularize the worship of Krishna through bhakti. The concept of the worship of Krishna based on bhakti cult was nothing new that he preached. However, it cannot be denied that Krishna was exalted to a supreme position during his time. That is why the followers of his School were greatly devoted to Krishna in the eighteenth century. The striking similarity can be noticed between the teachings of Chaitanya and that of Nimbarka. Both of them popularized the worship of Krishna and his consort Radha. The worship of Krishna accompanied by song and dance became widely prevalent. The devotees of both Nimbarka and Chaitanya schools of Vaishnavism in Manipur began to popularize Krishna-Radha cult and started putting the ritualistic or sectarian marks on their forehead. During the time of Garib Niwaz, Chaitanya School of Vaishnavism was more popular than other schools of Vaishnavism. The religion and culture of Manipur still bears the stamp of Chaitanya cult of Vaishnavism.

In order to popularize the Chaitanya cult of Vaishnavism, King Garib Niwaz constructed a temple in Saka 1644 = CE 1722 and dedicated it to Lord Krishna. The strict measures were adopted to maintain the sanctity of the Hindu deities.[35] The said temple still stands at Nahabam Brahmapur Leikai near the Krishna temple of Charairongba's time at Brahmapur Guru Aribam Leikai.

J. Shakespear (Political Agent in Manipur from 1905 to 1914, and an authority on the Religion of Manipur) is absolutely justified in stating that the devotedness of the king and the people to Krishna, regard for the learnedness of the brahmanas and respect for them in the society, and the zeal and enthusiasm of the people to protect the Hindu religion and culture furnish a solid evidence to the acceptance of Hinduism in Manipur.[36]

Garib Niwaz's period was very eventful from the perspective of the worship of the Hindu god Krishna and goddesses Kali and Durga, and the events that followed. The chronicle bears testimony to the fact that in CE 1726 a large tank called Ningthem Pukhri at Wangkhei Leikai, Imphal, was excavated for placing the stone images of Krishna and Kali in it which was a part of the consecration ceremonies[37]. J. Shakespear has revealed the fact that in 1906 these two images were found at the foot of the consecration post in the exact position when the tank was drained.[38] The chronicle also refers to the temple of Kalika (a Devi) built at Ningthem Pukhri. The members of Sairem family inhabiting this area used to worship the goddess in the temple.[39] There is also an evidence to show that a temple was dedicated to goddess Durga by King Garib Niwaz at Heibok hill.[40] We also learn from the chronicle that the Panthoibi was worshipped by the brahmanas during his time. The goddess was earlier worshipped by the traditional priests and priestesses called *Maibas* and *Maibis* respectively.[41] The worship of the goddesses–Kali, Durga and Panthoibi-testifies to the prevalence of the shakti cult of Hinduism concurrently with Vaishnava cult in the early eighteenth century.

In his bid to impose Hinduism on the common people and in order to establish the supremacy of Hindu gods and goddesses over the indigenous ones worshipped before the declaration of the Vaishnava form of Hinduism as the state religion, king Garib Niwaz destroyed the images of many traditional deities. Some temples of the indigenous deities were also demolished. Some of the traditional deities were burnt in the sacred grove and some were buried in the forest of Mongbahanba (now called Mahabali).[42] But in spite of that, the worship of the traditional gods–Laiwa-Haiba popularly known as Sanamahi continued with that of Krishna and Kali about which several instances are cited in the native chronicle.[43]

With the appointment of the guru as preceptor to the king, the influence of the traditional priests and priestesses gradually began to decline in the Meitei society. This sometimes resulted in the conflict between the representatives of the ancient faith and those of the new both on political and religious grounds.[44]

The attitude of king Garib Niwaz to the traditional religion was very much hostile. The king, however, did not destroy it completely which can fairly be attested to by the fact that some of the traditional gods were placed under the supervision and control of the brahmanas. The native chronicle supplies us with a very interesting piece of information in this regard. We learn from the chronicle that on the one hand the king destroyed a large number of traditional gods in CE 1723 but on the other he appointed brahmanas to initiate the worship of four traditional deities, namely, Lainingthou Nongshaba, Yumthei Lai, Panthoibi and Taibang Khaiba (sanamahi). But again Nongshaba, Panthoibi, and Sanamahi were destroyed along with many other gods and goddesses in CE 1726.[45] Thus we find that Hinduism and old religious faith sometimes coexisted and sometimes stood against each other. Both syncretism of and conflict between two different faiths were witnessed during the time of the king. The domination of one over the other or the subordination of one to other constitutes one of the distinguishing hallmarks of the religious history of Manipur of his time. However, his reign marked a departure to a great extent from the age-old faith and ultimately saw the dominance of Hinduism over the indigenous religion.

In pursuit of his religious orthodoxy, dogmatism and fanaticism, Garib Niwaz got a number of local *Puyas* and other ancient texts written by various Pandits of Manipur in old Manipuri script dealing with traditional religion, particularly Sanamahi, burnt to ashes. As far as our knowledge goes, 120 such works were consigned to flame. It will not be an exaggeration to say that he was more a destroyer than a protector of old faith, and a guardian of new faith.

The protagonists of the traditional religion raised their voice of protest against the forcible Hinduisation of the common people or imposition of Hinduism on them but it was suppressed by the king. The people not following the brahmanical code of conduct and the caste rules during his time were severely punished and sometimes sent into exile. Many innocent peoples became the victims of the repressive measures adopted by the king for the imposition and consolidation of Hinduism in the early part of the eighteenth century. Those who refused o join the fold of Hinduism were subjected to repression and oppression. The fact remains that Hinduism was made popular more by imposition than by persuasion during the time of king Garib Niwaz. W. McCulloch (Political Agent in Manipur from 1844 to 1867, and one of the authorities on the history of Manipur) remarked. "Hindu religion has been professed not from conviction, and it is but a fashion."[46] It cannot be accepted in toto. It is only partly true from the perspective of opposition faced by the said king in the wake of the introduction of Hinduism.

There was, of course, substantial progress in the field of adoption of Vaishnava form of Hinduism, but on the other hand, the king faced opposition from the votaries of indigenous religion. The period of Garib Niwaz, truly speaking, was that of progress and protest.

The Vaishnava Missionaries of different schools came to Manipur from Bengal to preach their respective Vaishnava faith and to carry on the proselytizing work. The famous Vaishnava preacher Shanti Das Goswami, who belonged to Ramanandi School, came to Manipur all the way from Sylhet with two of his followers, Bhagavan Das and Narayan Das, in or after 1722 but not later than 1728, to popularize the worship of Rama, Sita and Hanuman. It was under his influence that King Garib Niwaz became the follower of Ramanandi School of Vaishnavism in 1729.[47]

It is to be noted here that Ramananda (fourteenth century) like Nimbarka (CE 1114-1162), Ramanuja (early twelfth century), Chaitanya (CE 1485-1533) and Madhavacharya (CE 1199-1278) was also an exponent of Vaishnavism. He for the first time conceived of Rama and Sita as the dual incarnation of Vishnu. Those who accepted this form of Vaishnavism became the followers of his school.

The followers of Ramanandi School of Vaishnavism worshipped Rama as the principal deity. The images of Rama and Sita were installed in a temple built by Garib Niwaz in 1729 by the side of Ningthem Pukhri at Wangkhei Liekai, Imphal. The images are still worshipped in the temple now called Ramajiprabhu temple. In 1729 itself, an image of Hanuman was carved out of a big slab of stone and installed in a brick temple constructed by him at Mahabali. The Hanuman temple (also called Mahabali temple) still draw a huge crowd of devotees.[48]

During the period falling in between CE 1729 and 1737, the king and his three hundred followers were initiated to Ramanandi cult of Vaishnavism which can be testified to by the evidence recorded in the chronicle.[49]

The importance of Ramanandi cult in Manipur and the worship of Rama as a chief deity during the reign of Garib Niwaz can very well be proved by the numismatic and epigraphic evidence. Some of the bell metal coins of Garib Niwaz in both Nagari (Devanagari) and Bengali scripts bear the words. *"Je Shri Rama"*, *"Jaya Rama"*, and *"Ramu"*.[50] The first and the last line of the Ningel stone Inscription (dated Saka 1665 = CE 1743) of king Garib Niwaz in archaic Manipuri script and Manipuri language also refer to *"Jaya Shree Gariba nawaja Maharacha"* (Jaya Shri Gariba Nawaja Maharaja) and *"Rama Rama"* respectively.[51]

One of the distinguishing features of the religious history of medieval Manipur was the adoration of several Hindu deities at a time, notably, Rama, Krishna and Kali. This may precisely be attributed to the faith of the people in different sects of Hinduism.

It is worthwhile to note that only for some time king Garib Niwaz shifted his allegiance from Chaitanya sect to Ramanandi Sect of Vaishnavism. In fact, he extended his patronage more to the former than to the latter. He remained throughout devoted to Chaitanya Vaishnavism. The general acceptance of this form of Vaishnavism can be amply substantiated by the popularity it gained during his time. The royal chronicle contains some information regarding the persecution of the Ramanandis in CE 1731, 1734 and 1736.[52] The persecution of the followers of both the sects–Nimandi (named after Nimbarka) and the Ramandi (named after Ramananda)–in CE 1740 and 1742 is supported by local tradition.

During the time of king Garib Niwaz, both the schools of Vaishnavism–Chaitanya School and Ramanandi School flourished side by side but as rival sects. The former ultimately triumphed over the latter. The Ramanandi cult of Hinduism, however, did not completely die down. It rather continued to survive.

Garib Niwaz reigned up to CE 1748.

On the whole, the first half of the eighteenth century (which covers the periods of king Charairongba and Garib Niwaz) proved to be a blooming period in the history of the growth of Hinduism in Manipur.

Maramba alias Gour Shyam (the grandson of Garib Niwaz), who ruled the state first from CE 1753 to 1759 and then from 1762 to 1763, was a great votary of Shri Krishna. He used to worship the image of "Shri Radha-Raman" which after his demise was taken by one of his junior queens to Navadvipa (modern Nadiya in West Bengal) where she carried on the worship. This indicates that Gour Shyam too followed Chaitanya sect of Vaishnavism.

The reign of Gour Shyam's younger brother Jai Singh popularly known as Rajarshi Bhagyachandra (CE 1759-62, and 1763-98) ushered in a new era in the history of the growth of Chaitanya cult of Vaishnavism in Manipur. By restoring this cult of Vaishnavism based on the doctrine of *bhakti* or devotion and Bhagavata tradition to its pristine preeminent position, by initiating himself and his subjects into it and by accepting Vaishnava form of Hinduism as the State religion and consolidating it further he left behind a mark of his personality on the religion-cultural history of contemporary Manipur.

Jai Singh was initiated to Chaitanya sect of Vaishnavism by Shri Rupa Paramananda Thakur whose identity is not known to us nor do we know the exact year of the initiation of king. Several Vaishnava Missionaries associated with the school of Chaitanya as well as the followers of Madhavacharya sect of Gaudiya Vaishnavism visited Manipur at the invitation of king. In due course of time, the king became familiar with the concept of the worship of Krishna based on *bhakti* cult.

Bhagyachandra Maharaja was in frequent contacts with the Goswamis of Bengal. In or about 1777, the king and his subjects began to worship Radha and Krishna after coming under the influence of Narottam, a great saint of Chaitanya School of Vaishnavism or of Gauranga Parivar of the Bengal branch of Madhu Guru (Madavacharya) sect of the Vaishnava Sampradaya. Some of his subjects had already become followers of Chaitanya or Gauranga Mahaprabhu of Navadvipa and the cult of Radha-Krishna.[53]

There are some numismatic evidence to confirm the devotion of king Bhagya Chandra to Shri Govindaji (a manifestation of Krishna) during the second term of his rule (1763–98). The two gold coins bearing the legends in Sanskrit and the script in Nagari were issued by him, one in Saka 1691 = CE 1769 and the other in Saka 1694 = CE 1772. The first one depicts the legend on the reverse side which runs as follows: *"Shrimad Radha Govinda padaravinda makaranda madhukarasya"*, and the second one depicts on the reverse side *"Shri Shri Govinda pada suman madhukarasya"*. One of his silver coins also depicts *"Shri Govinda Deva"* on the reverse side.[54]

The image of Shri Govindaji was carved by an artisan named Sapam Lakshman Singh at Bishnupur palace in CE 1776 and was installed in Govindaji temple built at Canchipur (Langthabal) in 1779. In the same year, Bhagyachandra Maharaja shifted his capital from Bishnupur to Canchipur. The installation ceremony of Shri Govindaji was held on November 11, 1779 with ceremonial pomp and cultural show. On the occasion of ceremony, a five-day *Rasa-Lila* dedicated to Lord Krishna was performed for the first time in the *Rasa Mandal* at Canchipur, as described in the native chronicles. The popular tradition also affirms it. It may be added here that in *Rasa-Lila* the role of Krishna and his consort Radha is enacted. Besides the said image, other images of Shri Govindaji (Shri Krishna) were made. The chronicle refers to the carving of total six wooden images of Govindaji.[55] Of the six, the two images known as Vijay Govinda and Gopinath were worshipped at Sagolband and Ningthoukhong respectively.[56]

It may also be noted here that the image of Govindaji was worshipped by the kings and people of Manipur for several generations.

From the chronicle it appears that an image of Lord Jagannatha was also brought to Manipur and worshipped. The chronicle records some important events that took place in CE 1777 and 1784 in connection with the association of the royal family with that God.[57]

The chronicle also confirms the worship of the idol of Govindaji together with traditional deities by the king, brahmanas and others.[58] Both Hinduism and indigenous religion were patronized by the king.

The native chronicle bears the reflection of the truth that Ramanandi School of Vaishnavism had not lost the popularity completely in post-Garib Niwaz's times. From the available indication it can be deduced that inspite of all the attempts made by King Garib Niwaz to persecute the followers of that school, the arrival of Ramanandis in Manipur further continued between CE 1783 and 1792. The king (Bhagyachandra) himself created an image of

Rama before setting out on his pilgrimage to Vrindaban towards the end of his reign.[59] There is also an archaeological evidence to confirm the worship of Hanuman during his time. One inscribed stone with the carving of Hanuman erected at the entrance of the western gate of Kangla (site of the old royal palace, and the seat of the government till the reign of last independent king Kulachandra CE 1890-91)[60] proves that this image was also worshipped. The purpose of carving of the image of Hanuman was to ward off evil spirits from entering the palace compound at Kangla. We, however, do not find any such evidence which goes to prove the popularity of Ramanandi cult of Hinduism during his time. It is a fact to be reckoned with that the Vaishnavism of Chaitanya School remained domainant throughout the period. Shri Krishna acquired more popularity than Rama as the supreme deity. The people in the valley of Manipur were devoted to the worship of Radha and Krishna than to that of Rama and Hanuman at that time. The religion of Manipur still bears the stamp of Chaitanya School of Vaishnavism.

It was during the reign of Bhagyachandra that Hinduism was consolidated. J. Shakespear has also admitted that inspite of the successive Burmese invasion of Manipur during the time of that king,

Hinduism gained a firmer ground and stronger hold.[61]

It is striking to note that Maharaja Bhagyachandra had equal respect for Hinduism and indigenous religion because of his catholicity and magnanimity. He followed the policy of religious toleration. The worship of both traditional and Hindu deities during his time is beautifully illustrated in the native chronicle. The evidence recorded in it irrefutably proves that the image of Govindaji as well as the image of the popular household deity, Sanamahi, were worshipped concurrently by the people during his time. The Sanamahi cult retained its popularity. The common people, the brahmanas, the followers of Ramanandi cult and Chaitanya cult, and the followers of indigenous religious cults–all equally enjoyed the royal patronage or received an equal treatment at the hands of the king. The king worshipped not only the Hindu gods and goddesses such as Lord Rama, Sita, Hanuman, Krishna and Kali but also indigenous gods and goddesses like Sanamahi, Panthoibi, Leimaren, Pakhangba, Nongshaba and other deities with no lesser degree of veneration.[62] The image of God Sanamahi which he got sculptured in CE 1778 is still worshipped by the people of Manipur at the historical Sanamahi temple at Imphal. During the time of the king, some traditional deities were also identified with Hindu deities as a result of complete Hinduisation in the valley of Manipur. As for instance, Nongpok Ningthou of Koubru became God Shiva and Lairembi of Hiyangthang goddess Kamakhya. The traditional mode of worship of the Meitei god also underwent considerable changes. The whole religio-cultural pattern underwent profound changes during his time.

Bhagyachandra's period in reality witnessed a religious transformation and cultural synthesis. The religious system prevailing during his time was more or less a synthesis of religious beliefs of the Hindus and age-old traditional religious beliefs or a syncretism of old and new faiths. The system prevailing today in Manipur valley can be taken as a legacy of syncretized form of Hinduism that evolved during his time.

Suniti Kumar Chatterji has also observed that "...the introduction of Hinduism marked the synthesis of old and new elements, and consequently, it led to the evolution of a syncretised form of Hinduism which is still practiced here in Manipur."[63]

There is an evidence to prove that the celebration

of Durga Puja began for the first time on a large scale during the time of Bhagyachandra.[64] The said puja was no doubt first celebrated in Charairongba's time but not on a large scale.

The introduction of a new form of dance–*Rasa* (Radha–Krishna dance plays)–greatly based on the most popular traditional ritualistic dance called *Laiharaoba* (literally meaning the pleasing or rejoicing of God) during the time of Bhagyachandra is also worth-noting here. The first Manipuri *Rasa* dance was performed in November 1779 on the occasion of the intallation ceremony of the image of Shri Govindaji at Canchipur, as stated before. This dance later found a place in the six schools of Indian classical dance. "The Meitheis are now staunch Hindus, and through them Manipur has been made the easternmost outpost of Hindu culture in India. In modern times, the Manipur Vaishnava dance–the *Rasa*—has been a great contribution to the art of the Dance as an expression of Modern Indian culture," observes Suniti Kumar Chatterji.[65] Along with newly introduced *Rasa* dance the old dances guided by Manipuri dance gurus and pandits were also performed.

"Rajarshi Bhagyachandra also introduced a new style of Kirtan singing known as the *Nata Samkirtan* symbolising the highest form of surrender worship and ecstatic prayer enabling the devotees to have a direct communion with Shri Krishna. Since the time of this King, the *Nata–samkirtan* tradition has continued unabated throughout the valley and beyond in Vaishnava—Sampradaya area of Assam, Bengal and even Uttar Pradesh."

Bhagyachandra's time not only saw the emergence of a new syncretic religion but also introduction of new forms of dance and song. Manipur has undoubtedly made a significant contribution to the evolution of Hindu culture in India through her Vaishnavism, her dance and music, her art and culture and her literature.

The intensive orientation towards Hindu culture through Bengal Vaishnavism started from the time of Garib Niwaz onwards.

The religious and cultural integration of Manipur with India began in the time of Garib Niwaz and was consolidated by his grandson Rajarshi Bhagyachandra. Manipur became integrated with India from religious and cultural points of view during the time of the latter. It was also from his time that the Manipuri Hindus began to look towards the other regions of India for undertaking pilgrimage for fulfillment of their religious aspirations. Regular pilgrimage to Navadvipa (Nadiya) in West Bengal, Puri in Orissa, and Vrindavan in Uttar Pradesh commenced which in turn brought about an emotional integration of Manipur with India.

Maharaja Bhagyachandra died near Murshidabad in October 1798 before reaching his destination, Vrindavan. With his death an eventful era in the history of Hinduism in Manipur came to an end, but it will always be remembered that during his reign of nearly four decades Hinduism entered upon a new phase of orientation. His reign period was no doubt a glorious epoch in the religious and cultural history of Manipur.

Suniti Kumar Chatterji has strongly advocated the religious and cultural integration of Manipur with India. He has unequivocally stated that the harmonization or integration which has been going on in India since ancient times forming a single culture was also at work in Manipur and it can be seen from the syncretization of old and new faiths and tenets.[66]

Labanyachandra's period (CE 1798-1801) also saw a syncretization of old and new religious beliefs. There is a numismatic evidence to show the popularity of Krishna cult in the early part of his rule. The gold coin issued by the King in Saka 1721

= CE 1799 bearing the legend in Sanskrit in Nagari script on the reverse side : "*Shrimad Radha Govinda padaravinda makaranda madhukarasya*"[67] clearly shows his devotion to Radha and Govinda. It was during his time that the traditional Sanamahi cult and the worship of household deities were revived.[68] The traditional and Hindu deities received an equal amount of attention from the king. The traditional deities like Pakhangba, Sanamahi, Nongpok Ningthou and Panthoibi were worshipped even by the followers of Hinduism. With the identification of the goddess Panthoibi with Durga and that of Nongpok Ningthou with Shiva the traditional Meitei religion came under the Hindu influence to a considerable degree. The Hindu rituals were also adopted in worshipping the traditional deities. By the end of the rule of the king the assimilation of brahmana communities into the Meitei community was completed. They became part and parcel of Meitei society, and their marriage to Meitei women was formalized.

It appears from the chronicle[69] that King Madhuchandra (CE 1801-03) was also devotee of Shri Govindaji.

There are some numismatic evidence to confirm the popularity of Radha-Govinda cult during the times of kings Chourajit (CE 1803-13), Marjit Singh (CE 1813-19) and Jai Singh (CE 1822).

The gold coin issued in Saka 1731 = CE 1809 by king Chourajit depicts the legend in Sanskrit in Nagari script: "*Shrimad Radha Govinda padaravinda makaranda manomadhukarasya.*" And three silver coins of different denominations issued in Saka 1726 = CE 1804, Saka 1729 = CE 1807 and Saka 1734 = CE 1812 by him depict the legends. "*Shri Shri Radha Govinda apada sevaka*", "*Shri Radha Govinda padabja mano madhukarasya*", and "*Shrimad Radha Govinda padaravinda makaranda mano madhukar* as *ya*" respectively.[70]

The engraving of an image of Lord Govinda standing in tribhanga pose, playing on flute, and depiction of the legend in Sanskrit in Nagari Script : "*Shri Shri Radha Govinda padaravinda mano madhukarasya*" on one of the gold coins issued in Saka 1741 = CE 1819 by king Marjit Singh also proves the popularity of the worship of Radha and Govinda during his time.

Jai Singh II was also votary of Radha and Govinda. The depiction of Shri Radha-Govinda in tribhanga pose on the reverse side of the gold coin issued by him in CE 1822[72] also goes to prove the popularity of the cult of Radha-Govinda in early nineteenth century.

During the time of Maharaja Gambhir Singh (CE 1825-34) the famous temple at Canchipur, the new capital of Manipur, was dedicated to Lord Govindaji. According to J. Johnstone (Political Agent in Manipur, 1877-86, and an authority on the history of Manipur), the king took all possible care of Govindaji temple[73]. From the chronicle it distinctly appears that in November 1827 an image of Govindaji was brought back from Cachar where it was taken in CE 1819 by king Marjit at the time of fleeing away from Manipur because of the Burmese invasion. The image was installed in the Govindaji temple at Canchipur again. The worship of the image of Govindaji was popularized.[74] The brick temple, which was dedicated to Radha Raman (Govindaji), was constructed by Gambhir Singh at Canchipur.[75] The temple still stands on the hill-top of Canchipur but without any idol.

From the native chronicle and other sources we learn that it was during the reign of Gambhir Singh that the wooden images of Lord Jagannath, Balabhadra and Subhadra were installed for the first time in Manipur. He also founded an image of boy Krishna (Balagopal) and an image of boy Balaram (the elder brother of the former). He is also credited with having introduced an important religious festival known as *Rathayatra*. A new form of dance-drama associated with music called *"Sanjenba"* displaying the heroic activities of Shri Krishna and Balaram while tending cows was also introduced during his time. The concept was based on the theme of *Shrimad Bhagavat*.[76]

It may be added here that the images of Radha-Krishna, Krishna-Balaram, and Balabhadra-Subhadra are still worshipped in the famous Govindaji temple in the palace compound at Imphal built during the reign of Churachand Maharaja (CE 1891-1941). All Hindu temples in Manipur are still looked after by the brahmanas.

Gambhir Singh was a true devotee of Shri Krishna. During his time, Radha and Krishna (Govinda) cult of Hinduism was very popular in Manipur. The numismatic evidence also confirms the popularity of this cult in the early part of the nineteenth century. The gold coin issued by the said king in Chandrabda era of 1043 = Saka 1753 = CE 1831 depicting the legend on the obverse side in Sanskrit in Bengali script–*"Shri Radha Govinda Charana sevakasya"* (a devotee at the foot of celebrated Radha and Govinda)–proves that the king was a devotee of Radha and Govinda.[77]

According to an epigraphic evidence, King Gambhir Singh had faith in the worship of other deities too.[78]

The worship of Hindu gods and goddesses, particularly Radha and Govinda, further continued during the times of the successors of king Gambhir Singh. In CE 1846, Maharaja Nara Singh built a temple at Kangla and dedicated it to Shri Govindaji (Krishna) and his consort. The temple was, however, damaged along with the deities inside during the great earthquake of March 1868. It was reconstructed into present form by Maharaja Chandrakirti in 1869.[79] The engraving of the images of Lord Govinda and His divine consort Radha in tribhanga pose on the reverse side of one of the gold coins issued by King Nara Singh further attests to his devotion to these two Hindu deities. The coin depicts the legend in Sanskrit in Nagari script.

Hinduism in Manipur reached the zenith of its progress by the end of the nineteenth century.

Different schools of Vaishnavism, notably Madhavacharya School, Chaitanya School, Ramanandi School and School of Goudiya Vaishnavism flourished in Manipur during the eighteenth and nineteenth centuries. But, as already stated, Chaitanya School became most popular. The Krishna-Radha cult continued to maintain its popularity. The present Vaishnavism is, of course, a synthesis of different elements advocated by the followers of different schools of this religion. However, it is Chaitanya Vaishnavism which occupies the most prominent place in the history of Hinduism in Manipur.

The worship of Radha and Krishna in Manipur valley is still widely prevalent. The predominance of Radha-Krishna cult of Hinduism based on the doctrines of Chaitanya, Nimbarka and Madhavacharya schools is still discernible.

The contribution Manipur has made to the evolution of Hindu culture through her Vaishnavism will go down in the history of Hinduism in India.

IV

Brahmanisation that became very helpful in the growth of Hinduism in the valley of Manipur during the period also deserves our attention.

The immigration of brahmanas into Manipur from different parts of India in successive waves began during the reign of the famous King Kyamba *alias* Chintamani (CE 1467-1508) and continued down to the time of Gambhir Singh (CE 1825-34) with some break particularly in between 1798 and 1824. During the period, a large number of brahmanas migrated from Mathura, Vrindavan, Nandagrama, Kanyakubja (Kanauj), Kanpur and Prayag in Uttar Pradesh, Magadha in Bihar, Navadvipa (Nadiya), Krishnagar (or Krishnanagar) and Shantipur in West Bengal, Shrihatta (Sylhet) and Dhaka in eastwhile East Bengal, Puri in Orissa, Assam, Tripura, Nepal, Gujarat, Lahore in Western Punjab and other places to Manipur, settled in its valley, got absorbed into the Meitei society, became part and parcel of their community, got social recognition, enjoyed the royal patronage, received different family titles and *Gotras* (*salais*), and married local (Meitei) women whose offspring became the progenitors of many brahmana families of today, as recorded in the native chronicles,[80] some original works on the subject including an unpublished genealogical record,[81] and other reliable sources[82] of great historical value.

Besides the brahmanas, many kshatriyas and other Hindus also came to Manipur from eastern parts of India during the period and they like the former merged with the Meiteis.

The brahmanas who came and settled in Manipur during the time of King Charairongba belonged to Tripura, Puri (Orissa), Mathura, Nandagram, Navadvipa and other places.[83]

The Hinduization in the time of Garib Niwaz gave fillip to the immigration of brahmanas into Manipur. The forefathers of Manipuri brahmanas (locally called Bamon) bearing the family titles Gotimayum, Anoubam and Hanjabamayum, Hidangmayum, Brahmachari-mayum and Anoubam, Gopalhanjabamayum and Hajarimayum, and Sanjukimayam came from Shantipur and Jagannathbari (West Bengal), Kanyakubja (Uttar Pradesh), Sonardvipa (West Bengal), Barahanagar (West Bengal), Tripura and Sylhet respectively.[84] The royal chronicle records that thirty-nine brahmana gurus came to Manipur from neighbouring and far distant places during his time.[85] The coming of the brahmanas resulted in the making of a pluralistic society. These brahmanas greatly contributed to the intellectual, cultural and spiritual development of those dwellers of Manipur valley who came under their influence.

During the time of King Bhagyachandra, brahmanas came from Tripura, Bentala (Assam), Krishnanagar (West Bengal) and other places.[85]

Arrival of the brahmanas from as far as Vrindavan and Lahore continued. The royal chronicle specifically mentions the coming of monks and sanyasis in CE 1780.[87]

During the time of Gambhir Singh, there was an immigration of a large number of brahmanas into Manipur from Tripura, Brajabhumi (Mathura and Vrindavan) and east Bengal (Sylhet). The ancestors of the Manipuri brahmanas bearing the family titles Anoubam, Brajamayum (for having the name of Braja), and Acharyamayum (for performing *yajna* of the king) came from Tripura (also from Nandagrama), Vrindavan (via Shantipur) and Dhaka respectively and settled in Manipur valley during his time[88]. According to an authoritative work on the subject, only six brahmanas came to Manipur one each from Vrindavan, Mathura, Cachar, Dhaka, Agartala (Tripura) and Gangatir (not identified) during his time.[89]

The brahmanas who migrated to Manipur during the period settled down in different localities in its valley and carried on their proselytizing activities. They began to propagate the brahmanical religion and culture on a large scale which paved the way for the rise and growth of Hinduism which was declared the state religion in early eighteenth century, as stated before. A large number of Meiteis came within the fold of brahmanical Hinduism. They adopted the brahmanical way of life and mode of worship. Brahmanisation which accelerated the pace of Hinduism brought about many changes in the social, religious and cultural life of the Valley people. The gradual expansion of brahmanical culture resulted in the social and religious transformation in the valley of Manipur.

As a result of introduction of brahmanical culture, the traditional social customs, religious beliefs and practices, and rites, and rituals were gradually modified. The brahmanas performed religious ceremonies and conducted the rites and rituals along with the old family priests called *Maibas*. In fact, they were the joint custodians of socio-cultural tradition.

McCulloch's view, that the "Brahmans" did not command any respect in the Meitei society and their doctrines were not widely accepted, [90] can be dismissed as unworthy of credence. The brahmanas, no doubt, occupied an important position in the Meitei society but their supremacy was not acknowledged.

It is worthy of note that the absorption of newly immigrant brahmanas into the existing Meitei society led to the assimilation of religious ideas based on brahmanical tradition into the ideas of the Meiteis based on their age-old religious and cultural tradition which gave birth to a new syncretic culture. The brahmanic and Vaishnava doctrines got assimilated into or harmonized with the old faiths and beliefs of the Meiteis. The synthesis of two cultures–the indigenous and brahmanical–was maintained throughout the period of our study. Both the cultures flourished side by side. Some of the traditional gods and goddesses were, no doubt, identified with the deities of Hindu pantheon, but their worship went on concurrently with that of the brahmanical ones.

We have sufficient evidence to prove that the brahmanic religion was not the only form of worship and philosophy in Manipur. There were popular deities and rites to which the brahmanas were not opposed and which they countenance when it suited them. What takes place in Manipur today took place then. When some indigenous deities became important owing to their popularity and acceptability of the people or localities with which they were connected, they were recognized by the brahmanas and admitted to their panthon. Both forms of worship—indigenous and brahmanic—despite their differences existed. Both were based on philosophical doctrines. Both reached the level usually attained by popular beliefs. The coexistence of Hinduism and indigenous religion is one of the characteristic features of the religio-cultural history of Manipur.

Suniti Kumar Chatterji has rightly pointed out that "As usual, approximation of the old Meithei religion to the Hindu Brahmanical one began with the identification of the gods of the two religions."[91] He further observes : "A syncretism of the old pre-Hindu Meithei religion, mythology and ritual with the Hindu Brahmanical religion, mythology and ritual started very early; and with the friendly co-operation of the *Maibas* and *Maibis* (priests and priestesses of the old Meithei religion) on the one hand and the Brahmans and Vaishnavas on the other for some centuries, gave to Manipur its own distinctive form of Hinduism."[92]

Hinduism, which was introduced in Manipur, is a fusion of the two religious traditions, one represented by classical Hinduism and other by primordial religion. The syncretism of the Meitei indigenous religion with its gods and goddesses, its myths and rituals, its legends and traditions, its beliefs and practices and its rites and ceremonies and the brahmanical faith, and Vaishnava

Hinduism with its special emphasis on the worship of Radha and Krishna constitutes the essence of Hinduism. It was, in fact, an amalgamation or union of two different schools of religious thought.

C.J. Lyall's observation, that "...in Manipur the older religious ideas still survive beneath the surface of the philosophical system borrowed from India, which are reflected to a large extent in the lives, sentiments and beliefs of the people,"[93] is really commendable.

It is significant to note that despite all the changes that took place in the social and religious life of the Meiteis following the rapid expansion of brahmanical culture, their age-old customs, traditions, religious beliefs and practices, and rites and rituals continued to survive. Their traditional religion based on animistic and non-Hindu cults flourished side by side with Hinduism. The worship of their indigenous gods and goddesses, prominently Sanamahi and Panthoibi, went on with that of Hindu deities or divinities (of mainly Shiva, Shakti and Vaishnava sects) like Vishnu, Shiva, Durga, Kali and Krishna or Govindaji. More or less the same system is prevalent today.[94]

Presenting a correct picture of the subject, T.C.

Hodson says that the religion of the "Meitheis"–the Vaishnavite Hindus–exists side by side with the earlier faith.[95] He further states that here we have the stately fabric of Hinduism with its elastic case of accommodation and indigenous system of animism. The old order of things has not passed away by any means and the *Maiba*–the priest of the animistic system–and the Brahmans lived together and had their own importance.[96] J. Shakespear is also justified in stating that Manipur figured as a Hindu state and Hinduism was the state religion, and along the side of Hinduism the worship of indigenous gods and goddesses of non-Hindu cults continued. The progress of Hinduism in Manipur was slow but it was achieved by a compromise with ancient faith.[97] This can best be qualified in the words of Suniti Kumar Chatterji : "Manipur Hinduism gradually became a synthesis of the old Meithei religion with gods and goddesses and myths, its own legends and traditions, its social customs and usages, and its priests and ceremonials, and of Brahmanical Hinduism with its special worship of Radha and Krishna."[98]

V

Hinduism left behind its impact on various

aspects of the life and culture of the Meiteis in the valley of Manipur.

There was social transformation as a sequel to the introduction of Hinduism.

It may first be noted here that there was neither any class nor any caste in the Meitei society before the introduction of Hinduism in the early part of the eighteenth century. But the coming of the brahmanas and kshatriyas to Manipur, and the mass conversion to Hinduism in the time of Garib Niwaz led to the formation of two distinct social classes—brahmanas and kshatriyas. The two-fold social division ultimately resulted in some sort of class or caste distinction. As they represented two upper classes, the feeling of low and high emerged in the society, and social distinction was maintained to some extent. Garib Niwaz along with his people of seven clans strictly followed the caste rules of the Hindus which can definitely be taken as a legacy of the brahmanas who were dominating the social and religious scene at that time.

According to some authorities, in CE 1714 Garib Niwaz adopted Hinduism and his people followed his example and since that date they observed the rules of caste and ceremonial unity with rigidity. Hinduism gained a remarkably strong hold on the people.[99] There was no doubt complete transformation of the old social order during his time.

It is undeniable that caste rule in some form or the other was followed during the time of Garib Niwaz. But it was an exception and not the rule. It was just a passing phase. The caste rule in the true sense of the words was never applied in post-Garib Niwaz times.

The caste system was not as much rigid in the Meitei society as in other Hindu society in India. The classes or castes as such did never exist in the Meitei society. The vaishyas and the shudras—the two other social classes—are till today conspicuous by their absence. The social hierarchy of the ancient Hindus was never maintained in the Meitei society. Manipur brand of Neo-Hinduism was totally different from the Hinduism in ancient India.

T.C. Hodson has correctly stated that "The Meitheis do not allow the supremacy of the Brahman, and none of the ordinary definitions of caste applies to their social order."[100] His statement is applicable to the social scenario that emerged after Garib Niwaz.

It is traditionally believed that after conversion to Hinduism all the Meiteis including members of the King's own family were declared to belong to the Kshatriya class. The royal dynasty in particular was identified with the *Suryavamsa* (solar dynasty) of Ikshvaku described in the *Valmiki-Ramayana* and puranas. "Thus Hinduised Meitei society became Virtually transformed into a single caste polity with descendants of immigrant brahmans belonging to the Brahman caste."

As a result of expansion of Hindu culture in Manipur valley several social changes took place. The Hindu influence went a long way in transforming the contemporary social and religious system. The customs observed, the rites and ceremonies performed and the festivals celebrated in conformity with the Hindu ideals and practices during the period deserve our special attention. T.C. Hodson has also pointed out that the traditional social customs, rites, rituals and ceremonies were greatly modified after the adoption of Hindu practices.[101]

The birth ceremonies in Manipur society are very much in line with the Vaishnava Hindu tradition. The marriage ceremonies were performed both according to Hindu and traditional rites. The restrictions imposed on marriage between the family of same *gotra* or *salai* was evidently the impact of Hinduism. Marriage within the same caste, sanctity of the *gotra* and the freedom granted to brahmanas in the society are also considered to be the legacy of Hinduism.[102]

The ceremony of taking the sacred thread (one of the sixteen samskaras of the Hindus from the birth to death) was first performed during the time of King Charairongba. The king himself took the sacred thread formally in CE 1704 after his conversion to Hinduism. From the native chronicle it appears that between CE 1717 and 1737 (Garib Niwaz's time) the sacred thread ceremonies were held at different occasions. The most positive evidence in this regard is that in CE 1737-38 three hundred people including the king (Garib Niwaz) took the sacred thread.[103] There are frequent allusions in the chronicle to the taking of sacred thread between CE 1784 and 1792 (Bhagyachandra's time).[104] The sacred thread was taken by both brahmanas and kshatriyas.

Some of the old Meitei customs underwent considerable changes as a result of the growing influence of Hinduism during the time of Garib Niwaz. The Hindu method of cremation was compulsorily adopted during his time for the disposal of the dead in place of burial, which was generally practiced in the so-called pre-Hindu period. The purification ceremony or *Shradha,* which is still in practice, was also a Hindu adoption. It was adopted by the brahmanas, kshatriyas and other Hindus. Despite the complete acceptance of Hinduism, the traditional social customs and practices went on side by side with Hindu practices. And the traditional priest (*Maiba*) continued to play his role and occupy his importance in the society along with the brahmana priest.[105]

As a sequel to the adoption of cremation system, the custom of Sati (one of the social evils) followed. The chronicle record a few instances of that custom practised between CE 1725 and 1740.[106] That evil practice, however, did not continue for long.

It is believed that altogether seven festivals were introduced in Manipur directly under the influence of Hinduism. Three of these, namely, Holi, Janmastami and Rathyathra are directly connected with Krishna whose worship became very popular after the advent of Chaitanya Vaishnavism in Manipur. The other Hindu festivals celebrated during the period include Durga and Kali Puja, and Diwali. All these festivals are still being celebrated by the Meitei Hindus in Manipur and outside.

It may also be added here that a number of

traditional festivals were modified or identified with concurrent Hindu festivals during the reign of King Garib Niwaz. Such festivals are spelt out in the archaic text *Sanamahi Laikon* the notable of which are the annual boat race festival, then traditionally known as *Heigsru-Hidongba* regularly held in the month of November, renamed as *Jalayatra,* the festival of *Waira Tenkap,* traditionally held in the month of February, redesignated as *"Kirtan of Lord Rama"*, the traditional festival of *Kongba Leithong Phatpa,* held in the month of March or April, identified with *Vishnu Samkranti,* the festival of *Ahong Khongching,* usually held in the month of July, substituted by *Dol Yatra,* the regular worship of *Nung-goibi* in the month of October, substituted by *Dasnam kwak-tanba* or *Dusserah,* and tasting of newly harvested rice known as *Chanou Huichintu,* held in the month of October, replaced by *Govardhan puja.*[107]

The linguistic change and literary progress also deserve our notice.

After the coming of the brahmanas—the speakers of Sanskrit language—from different parts of India to Manipur during the period, the Sanskrit language came into use. It is worth while to mention here that they not only encouraged the use of this language but also translated the Sanskrit books they brought along with them into Manipuri after acquiring the knowledge of this language. Some intellectuals and learned scholars belonging to Meitei community acquired the knowledge of Sanskrit after coming into contact with the neo-brahmanas. The tradition of acquiring knowledge of Sanskrit and translating some of the ancient Indian texts in that language into Manipuri and English was handed down from generation to generation in some Meitei families. The native Sanskrit scholars have made substantial contribution to the enrichment of the knowledge of the people of the land regarding the history and culture of India through their said translated works.

Likewise, after the coming of the Hindu missionaries–the votary of Chaitanya Vaishnavism–from Bengal to Manipur during the time of King Garib Niwaz, the strong champion of Hinduism, the Bengali language came into use the most notable example of which is the composition of the *Bijoy Panchali*–one of the native chronicles–by Kritichandra in that language under the patronage of that king. The said missionaries from Bengal played an active role in the introduction of Bengali script. They not only preached the doctrines of

Vaishnavism but also exercised their linguistic influence on the potentates and populace. Following the introduction of Hinduism, the Bengali script was adopted in place of archaic Meitei script. Some of the local chronicles and other works were composed in Manipuri language by using that script. It has been rightly pointed out that "...from the middle of the 18th century, they (the "Meitheis") adopted the Bengali script with the conversion of the ruling Manipur king Gharib - Nawaz Singh to Chaitanya Vaishnavism through Bengali Vaishnava preachers from Sylhet..."[108]

The newly introduced Sanskrit and Bengali had great bearings on coins, inscriptions and literature of Manipur.

The introduction of Hinduism, no doubt, marked the beginning of a new age in the history of Manipuri coinage. All the successors of King Charairongba down to the last independent King Kulachandra issued coins bearing the legends in Sanskrit either in Devanagari (also called Nagari) or Bengali script. The use of Sanskrit words in Devanagari and Bengali script on bellmetal, gold and silver coins from the time of King Garib Niwaz onwards bear eloquent testimony to the impact of Hinduism on the designs, patterns and styles of the coins. The use of the initial letters of the names of the issuing kings, for example, *"JE SHRI, GARIBNIWAJA MEKHLESHWAR"* and *"SHRI GAMBHEERA SIMHA NRIPAVA RASYA CHANDRABDA* 1043," and the depiction of names of the Hindu deities worshipped, for example, *"JE SHRI RAMA, JAYA RAMA"* and *"SHRI SHRI GOVINDA, SHRIMAD RADHA GOVINDA"* on different coins issued between CE 1709 and 1834[109] reflect the Hindu influence on the coins.

The gold coins issued by the kings between CE 1798 and 1822 depict the legends in Sanskrit in Nagari script showing the popularity of Radha and Govinda cult.[110] A gold coin of Gambhir Singh issued in Saka 1753 = CE 1831 depicting the legends in Sanskrit in Bengali script proves that the king was a devotee of Radha and Govinda.[111]

So was the impact of Hinduism on the inscriptions. We find the use of Sanskrit words *"Rama Rama"* in the last line and *"Jaya shri"* in the first line of Ningel stone Inscription of King Garib Niwaz (a great votary of Hinduism) in archaic Manipuri script and Manipuri language dated Saka 1665 = CE 1743.[112]

Both coins and inscriptions bear the stamp of Hindu influence.

The introduction of Hinduism in Manipur also

resulted in a great literary progress which was witnessed during the eighteenth and nineteenth centuries. The attention of the local writers was diverted towards producing those kinds of literature which could focus mainly on Hindu religion and culture. The primary objective behind such kind of motivation was to create awareness among the people about the richness of the Hindu culture and consciousness for preserving and promoting the newly introduced Vaishnava form of Hinduism.

From the time of King Garib Niwaz a new period began in the history of Manipuri literature. It was during his time that the two great epics–*Rāmāyaṇa* (in full) and *Mahābhārata* (in part)–were rendered into Manipuri. The entire *Rāmayāṇa* (a Bengali version) of Krittivasa (fourteenth century) popularly known as *Krittivasi Rāmāyaṇa* was rendered into Manipuri by Kshema Singh (who not merely knew Bengali but also had specialized in Rāmāyaṇa) with the help of five other poets. The *Adi, Virata* and *Ashvamedhika* parvans of the *Māhābharata* composed in Bengali in the sixteenth century by Gangadasa Sen was also translated into Manipuri by the local scholars well versed in Bengali language.

The reign of King Jai Singh generally called Bhagyachandra which brought in a great Vaishnava revival is also marked by the enrichment of Manipuri literature. The influence of Sanskrit on Manipuri literature was preponderant. This can be seen in the texts composed during his time. The Sanskrit words in combination with words of Manipuri origin were frequently used in the works written in his time. Though many of such works were destroyed by the Burmese in the course of the devastation of Manipur, but few were preserved which include prominently *Janmejaya sarpa yajna* (Janmejaya's snake sacrifice), *Ashvamedha* (Yudhisthira's horse sacrifice) and *Ashtakal Lila*) (Shri Krishna's round the clock sports). Later on, some treatises on Manipuri dance and music were also compiled both in Manipuri and Sanskrit.

It is also worthwhile to note that during the time of King Chourajit the *Bhāgavad Gitā* was rendered into Manipuri. *Dharani Saṁhitā*, a Sanskrit text, was compiled during the reign of King Gambhir Singh.

The rich Manipuri literature proved to be a potent force for the propagation and popularization of the Hindu religion and culture and rich cultural heritage of India among the masses. It may be mentioned here that particularly the Vaishnavite literature proved to be very helpful in promoting the further growth of Hinduism.

After the acceptance of the *Rāmayāṇa,* the *Mahābhārata,* the *Purāṇas* and other Sanskrit literature, Manipur fell in line with the rest of Hindu India. It became fully integrated with India through its Vaishnava form of Hinduism, rich literature, art and culture and so on. As already stated, Manipur became integrated with India only from religious and cultural points of view. The old myths and legends of the Manipuris after their Hinduisation also got linked up inextricably with brahmanical legends which resulted in the production of a veritable Manipur-Purāṇa in Sanskrit and in Manipuri. The traditions recorded in brahmanical and Puranic literature were reconciled with the Manipuri or Meitei traditions, history, legends and folk-lore.

Manipuri literature was ranked among the advanced literature of Hindu India.

The artistic history of Manipur embracing the art and architecture and sculpture and iconography was greatly affected by the new currents of Hinduism. The growth of Hinduism provided an impetus to the construction of temples. In the construction of the temples, a new Hindu style of architecture was adopted. During the period, the temples of Rama, Hanuman, Radha-Krishna, Govindaji, Kali and other Hindu gods and goddesses were constructed by following the different Hindu styles of architecture. It may further be mentioned here that the architectural style of Hindu temples in Manipur was greatly influenced by the contemporary schools of architecture and by its own traditional or conventional style.

The architectural style of Krishna temple built during the time of King Charairongba[113] is very much similar to that of Bengal school ascribed to the seventeenth and eighteenth centuries. It is said that this temple is the prototype of the "hut-type" or "vernicular Chala-type" temple of Bengal constructed during the period. It is believed that this style of architecture was introduced in Manipur by the brahmanas who mostly came from Bengal during his time as the religious missionaries championing the cause of Vaishnavism.[114]

The temple of Hanuman built during the time of King Garib Niwaz also bears resemblance to "hut-type" temples of contemporary Bengal. The architectural style of Hanuman temple of Mahabali and Krishna temple of Guruaribam Leikai constructed in the eighteenth century is more or less similar.[115] It must, however, be admitted that the architectural style of Bengal school was slightly modified by the local genius–architects (skilled in the art and science of building)—in Manipur.

The three temples known as temple of Pakhangba, temple of Yumjao Lairembi and temple of Nongshaba built in the Sylhet district of erstwhile east Bengal (now Bangladesh) (a half km away from the Manipuri Rajbari, then a capital site of the Manipuri king at Sylhet) during the time of Gambhir Singh bear such carvings, designs and motives which point to the syncretism of traditional and Hindu faith.[116]

In the beginning of the nineteenth century, several shrines or temples dedicated to Lord Shiva were constructed in Manipur. One such shrine of Shiva was constructed at Nongmaiching. The archaeological discovery of an image of Shiva in human form sculptured in sandstone and seated on a bull or Nandi and depicted with the Linga portion (kept on display in Mutua Museum, Imphal)[117] testifies to the prevalence or continuance of Shiva worship down to the nineteenth century. It is historically and archaeologically proven fact that both Shaiva and Shakti–the two popular religious cults of Hinduism–flourished side by side with Vaishnava sect of Hinduism in Manipur during the period.

The art of sculpture and iconography also thrived in Manipur as a result of introduction of Hinduism. The advent of Hinduism, no doubt, marked a new distinct phase in the history of sculpture and iconography in Manipur. The icons or images of three main sects of Hinduism–Shaiva, Shakti and Vaishnava–were sculptured in various forms by different sculptors during the eighteenth and nineteenth centuries which can be proved by the archaeological discovery of those sculptured images. All Hinduized Manipuri kings encouraged the sculptors by extending their patronage to them to carve the images of Hindu deities for promoting the growth of Hinduism.

The spread of brahmanical culture led to the transformation of old an iconic form of worship into an iconic one. The worship of icons of Hindu pantheon began from the fifteenth century onwards. The introduction of iconic form of worship necessitated the making of icons of Hindu deities. The images of Hindu gods and goddesses were carved out of stones and woods and installed in the newly constructed temples and at other sacred and historically important places for their worship which helped in the propagation of Hinduism.

The images of Rama, Sita and Hanuman (of Ramanandi sect of Vaishnavism), images of Krishna, Varaha and Narsi*ṁ*ha-all incarnations of Lord Vishnu–Balaram, Radha, Govindaji, Jagannath, Balabhadra and Subhadra (of Chaitanya, Madhavacharya and other sects of Vaishnavism), images of Durga and Kali (of the Shakti sect of Hinduism), the icons of Shiva, Ganesh and Karttikeya (of the Shiva sect), and the icons of other Hindu deities like Bhairava, Garuda, Dhruva, Prahlada and Sarasvati sculptured during the period are worth-mentioning here. The images were mostly seculptured in sandstone. Only few images were carved out of wood. The wooden images include those of Govindaji, Jagannath, Balabhadra and Subhadra. The images of Rama, Sita, Hanuman, Radha-Krishna, Govindaji (Krishna), Kali, etc installed in the temples during the period are still worshipped along with other deities by the Hindus. The artistic presentation of the icons of the Hindu pantheon does not exhibit the fine workmanship because of the local influence of the time.[118] The carving of the images of these Hindu deities shows that there were adherents of different sects of Hinduism.

Most of the icons/images mentioned above are preserved in Manipur State Museum and Mutua Museum, Imphal.

Manipuri dance, drama and music also felt the impact of Hinduism. A new form of dance known as *Rasa*, which is intimately connected with Chaitanya School of Vaishnavism, became very popular during the time of King Bhagyachandra. This dance later got recognition as one of the six prominent schools of Indian classical dance, as noted before. However, the old ritualistic dances like *Laiharaoba* of the so-called pre-Hindu period did not lose its importance. A new school of drama also came into being which was fundamentally based on the Vaishnavite themes. It was staged at different places under different names. The drama known as *Kaliyadaman* was staged at Canchipur and Kangla. The other two dramas came to be known as *Dhruva-charit* and *Harichandra*.

The brahmanas made significant contribution to the development of Manipuri classical music known as "*Nat*" based on six *ragas* and thirty-six *raginis* expounded in the Sanskrit texts of Indian classical music. The brahmanas well versed in musicology composed various types of song, including the devotional ones (based on *bhakti* cult), both in Sanskrit and Bengali. The worship of Lord Krishna accompanied by song and dance became widely prevalent. The concept of *Kirtan*, usually sung by the followers of Chaitanya Vaishnavism, also developed in Manipuri society. The singing of *Kirtan* in Bengali style commenced. During the time of King Bhagyachandra, who was a staunch follower of Chaitanya School of Vaishnavism, the songs and the *Kirtan* were composed in Bengali. And so is the case with the composition of the lyrics of *Rasa-lila*. All these developments took place in the course of expansion of Hindu culture in the valley of Manipur. The process of Sanskritization and syncretization reached its culmination by the end of the nineteenth century.

It is worthy of remark that some British scholars made an abortive attempt to distort the truth with regard to the impact of Hinduism on the life and culture of the people in the valley of Manipur during the eighteenth and nineteenth centuries.

T.C. Hodson says : "It is not sound to regard these beliefs as survivals despite the official superstratum of Hinduism which exists in Manipur solely in its exoteris form without any of the subtle metaphysical doctrines...It is difficult to estimate the precise effect of Hinduism on the civilization of the people, for to the outward observer they seem to have adopted only the festivals, the outward rituals, the caste marks, and the exclusiveness of Hinduism...In Manipur, where Hinduism is a mark of respectability, it is never safe to rely on what men tell of their religion...We are justified in holding them still to be animists."[119] He further asserts that Manipuri religion was Hindu only in form not in substance, that Hinduism of Manipur was more ritualistic than philosophical, and that the basic doctrines of Hinduism were conspicuous by their absence.[120] His arguments are not convincing and hence it can be disposed of W. McCulloch's statement, that the Hinduism of the Meiteis was purely superficial because of non–observance of Hindu customs, lack of respect for the brahmanas, etc,[121] can be dismissed as unworthy of acceptance. C.J. Lyall's remark, that "While Buddhism has profoundly modified the original animism, Manipur after coming within the pale of Hinduism has imposed upon itself burdensome restrictions of caste and ritual from which its greater neighbour is happily free."[122] is also not tenable.

The eighteenth and nineteenth centuries taken together may undoubtedly be regarded as blooming period in the history of evolution of Hinduism in Manipur.

Hinduism in Manipur during the period under notice had far-reaching impact on contemporary society, indigenous religion and culture, language and literature, art and architecture, sculpture and iconography, coins and epigraphy, and dance and music.

NOTES AND REFERENCES

1. *Cheitharol Kumbaba* (Hereinafter abbrev. as CK), ed. N. Khelchandra Singh and L. Iboongohal Singh (Imphal, 1967), p. 262.
2. *Sculptures of Manipur, Bulletin* No. 2 Mutua Museum (abbrev. as MM), Imphal, Dec. 1982.
3. R.K. Jhalajit Singh, *A Short Hisory of Manipur* (Imphal, 1965), p. 718.
4. CK, pp. 58-60.
5. "The Religion of Manipur", in *Transactions of the Folk-Lore Society* (abbrev. as TFLS), Calcutta, XXIV, 4, 1913.
6. "Konthoujam Lairemma Inscription," No. II cf *Epigraphical Records of Manipur* (abbrev. as ERM), I (MM, Imphal, 1986), pp. 2-3.
7. *The Religion of Manipur* (Beliefs, Rituals and Historical Development), Calcutta, 1980, pp. 184-85.
8. CK, p. 72.
9. *Ibid*, p. 75.
10. *Ibid.*
11. J. Shakespear, "The Religion of Manipur", TFLS, XXIV, 4, 1913, pp. 415-16.

12. *Kubjika Tantra* (MSS No. 3174), Royal Asiatic Society of Bengal, Patala-VII, also quoted in *Journal of the Royal Asiatic Society of Bengal, Letters,* XIV, 1948; *Pranatosani Tantra* (Vasumati ed), p. 234, quoted in D.C. Sircar, *The Sakta Pithas* (Delhi, 1973), p. 19.
13. *The Meitheis* (London, 1908, rept. Delhi, 1984), p. 102.
14. *Manipur Rock Carving and Inscriptions* (Abbrev. as MRCI), *Bulletin* No. 4 (MM, Imphal, Dec. 1984), p. 20.
15. "Heishnam Lairemma Inscription" (Stone inscription No. 2), Cf ERM, I (MM, Imphal, 1986), pp. 24-25.
16. CK, p. 260.
17. *OP. cit.*, pp. 103-04
18. *My Experiences in Manipur and the Naga Hills* (London, 1896, rept. Delhi, 1971), p. 145 f.
19. *Gazetteer of Manipur* (1886).
20. CK, pp. 199 ff, 263.
21. CK, p. 56; see also R.K. Jhalajit Singh, *op. cot.*, pp. 115-16 ; L. I. Singh, *An Introduction to Manipur* (Imphal, 1963), p. 209; K.B. Singh, "Manipuri Vaishnavism : A Sociologica Interpretation", *Sociological Bulletin,* Xii, 2,1963, pp. 66ff.
22. L.I. Singh, *op. cit.*, p. 32.
23. *Op. cit.*, p. 135.
24. *Op. cit.*, p. 132.
25. *Op. cit.*, pp. 141-42. She is of the view that "Brahmin

influence had been steadily at work in Manipur for sometime before the actual acceptance of Vaishnavite faith...It seems likely that there was a certain amount of Hinduising during the medieval period and identification of local with Hindu deities...While we allow for a certain degree of Hindu presence in Manipur before the time of Charairongba, We have no evidence that it was either very large or very vigorous." (*op.cit,* pp. 133-34.)

The view held by some native and outside scholars that Hinduism did not take its root in Manipur before the introduction of Vaishnavism and its declaration as the state religion in the eighteenth century can be disposed of in the light of the evidence available to us. The worship of Hindu gods and goddesses of Shaiva, Shakti and Vaishnava sects in Manipur began as early as the eighth century. (See W. Yumjao Singh, *Report on the Archaeological Studies in Manipur, Bulletin* No. 1 (Imphal, 1935), pp. 40-43, and Appendix I; also his *The Religious Belief of Ancient Manipur* (Imphal, 1966), pp. 28-29; S.K. Chatterji, *Kirata-Jana-Kriti* (The Asiatic Society, Calcutta, 1974), p. 48; also his *Religious and Cultural Integration of India* (Imphal, 1967), pp. 42-44, 48; M. Jhulon Singh, *Vijaya Panchali* (a chronicle of history of Manipur), Eng. trans. from *Bijoy Panchali* in Bengali by Kritichandra and compiled by Dvija Sita Ram Sharma, I (Imphal, 1936), p. 14; J. Shakespear, "The Religion of Manipur," TFLS, XXIV, 4, 1913, p. 19;

R.M. Nath, *The Background of Assamese Culture* (Shillong, 1948), pp. 86, 88.

The latter half of the fifteenth century and the early part of the sixteenth constituted another important phase in the history of the rise and growth of Hinduism in Manipur. The eighteenth and nineteenth centuries withnessed the spectacular progress of Hinduism. It further continues to be a popular religion in Manipur. The present work does not offer scope to go into further details of the subject.

26. *Encyclopaedia of Religion and Ethics* (abbrev. as ERE), VIII (New york, 1964), p. 402.
27. CK, p. 59.
28. See R.G. Bhandarkar, *Vaishnavism, Saivism and Minor Religious Systems* (Strassburg, 1913, rept. Varanasi, 1965), p. 62; Charles Eliot, *Hinduism and Buddhism: An Historical Sketch*, Vol. II (London, 1921, rept. 1957), p. 230.
29. *Coins of Manipur, Bulletin* No. 1 (MM, Imphal, October 1980), Catalogue II.
30. CK, pp. 58-60.
31. *Ibid*, pp. 59-60.
32. *Ibid.*, p. 66.
33. C.U. Aitchison, *A Collection of Treaties, Engagements and Sanads Relating to India and Neighbouring Countries*, XII (Calcutta, 1931), p. 102.
34. CK, p. 69; T.c. Hodson, *The Meitheis*, p. 45.
35. CK, p. 71.

36. "The Religion of Manipur", TFLS, XXIV, 4, 1913, p. 451.
37. CK, p. 75.
38. "The Religion of Manipur", TFLS, XXIV, 4, 1913, pp. 415-16.
39. CK, p. 75.
40. Kh. Kaomacha Singh, *Manipur Itivritta*, pp. 41-42 and 85.
41. CK, p. 72.
42. For details see CK, pp. 72-75; *Vijaya Panchali* (*supra*), pp. 65-66; N. Khelchandra Singh, "Manipurda Hindu Dharmagi Prabhab", *Souvenir of Manipur Rajya Hindu Sammelan* (abbrev. as SMRHS), Imphal, Dec. 1981, pp. 32-37; G. Kabui, *History of Manipur*, I (Precolonial Period), Delhi, 1991, p. 255.
43. CK, pp. 77-79.
44. Hodson, *op. cit.*, p. 94.
45. CK, p. 72; see also N. Khelchandra Singh, *Ariba Manipuri Sahityagi Itihasa* (Imphal, 1969), pp. 36-37; Kabui, *op. cit*.
46. *An Account of the Valley of Manipur and of the Hill Tribes* (selection from the Records of the Govt. of India No. XXVII), Calcutta, 1859, pp. 17-18.
47. See also *Vijaya Panchali* (*supra*), p. 65; Jhalajit Singh, *op.cit.*, pp. 134-36.
48. CK, pp. 77-78; also *Vijaya Panchali* (*supra*), pp. 65-68; Jhalajit Singh, *op.cit.*, p. 136.

49. CK, p. 83 f.
50. *Coins of Manipur, Bulletin* No. 1 (MM, Imphal, October 1980), Catalogue III-VIII; also P. Gunindro Singh, *Manipur Numismatic* (Imphal, 1983), pp. 7, 30-33.
51. ERM, I, pp. 8-13.
52. CK, pp. 79, 83-84.
53. L.I. Singh, *op.cit.*, pp. 32-33.
54. *Coins of Manipur, Bulletin* No. 1 (MM, Imphal, October. 1980), pp. 14-22; Gunindo Singh, *op. cit.*, pp. 58-59.
55. CK, pp. 117, 156.
56. Jhalajit Singh, *op.cit.*, pp. 165-66.
57. CK, pp. 130, 156, 158, 177.
58. *Ibid.*, p. 127.
59. *Ibid.*, p. 129.
60. MRCI, *Bulletin* No. 4 (MM, Imphal, Dec. 1984), pp. 8-9.
61. "The Religion of Manipur," TFLS, XXIV, 4, 1913, p. 444.
62. For details see CK, pp. 118, 127, 133 and 140.
63. *Religious and Cultural Integration of India*, p. 41.
64. See also MRCI, *Bulletin* No. 4 (MM, Imphal, Dec. 1984), p. 20.
65. *Kirata-Jana-Kriti*, p. 48.
66. For details see *Religious and Cultural Integration of India*, pp. 41-49.

67. *Coins of Manipur, Bulletin* No. 1 (MM, Imphal, October 1980), pp. 15-16.

68. CK, pp. 165-68.

69. *Ibid.*, p. 170.

70. *Coins of Manipur, Bulletin* No. 1 (MM, Imphal, Octob. 1980), pp. 17-18; Gunindro Singh, *op. cit.*, pp. 73-74.

71. *Coins of Manipur, Bulletin* No. 1. (MM, Imphal, October. 1980), p. 19.

72. *Ibid*, pp. 20-21.

73. *My Experiences in Manipur and the Naga Hills*, p. 88.

74. CK, p. 225.

75. L. Kunjeswori Devi, *Archaeology in Manipur* (Delhi, 2003), p. 122.

76. CK, p. 235; R.K. Sanahal, "Manipurda Vaishnava Dharma", pub. in *Shri Shri Radha Krishna Janmastami Celebrations*, ISKCON, Imphal, August 1986; Jhalajit Singh, *op.cit.*, p. 208, see also pp. 205-06; Johnstone, *op.cit.*

77. *Coins of Manipur*, Bulletin No. 1 (MM, Imphal, October 1980), p. 22; Gunindro Singh, *op. cit.*, p. 83.

78. "Heisham Lairemma Inscription" (Stone Inscription No. 2), ERM, I, pp. 24-25.

79. See also Kunjeswori Devi, *op. cit.*, p. 124.

80. CK, pp. 36, 56-58, 64f, 122, 129; *Vijaya Panchali* (*Supra*), pp. 85-87.

81. *Bamon Khunthoklon* (abbrev. as BK), ed. H. Ibopiskak Meitei (Imphal, 1987), pp. 3-11; Mss. *Bamon Meihaobarol* (without any page number).

82. L.I. Singh, *op. cit.*, pp. 31-33, 207-11, and Appendix III; Jhalajit Singh, *op. cit.*, pp. 82, 90, 95, 104, 113-16, 138, 167, 206; see also his "The Migration of Brahmins and its Impact on the culture of Manipur," *Proceedings of the North East India History Association* (Imphal, 1982), pp. 84-88; W. Ibohal Singh, *A History of Manipur* (early period), Imphal, 1986, pp. 74-81, 606-07.

    The name of the brahmanas and of the places from where they migrated to Manipur, the places of their settlements in Manipur valley, the family titles allotted to them with *gotras* (*salais*), name of the local women they married, etc are described in detail in the sources mentioned under reference nos. 59-61.

83. BK, pp. 7-9; W.I. Singh, *op.cit.*, pp. 578-80; L.I. Singh, *op.cit.*, pp. 209-10; Jhalajit Singh, *op. cit.*, pp. 115-16; CK, pp. 56-58.

84. BK, pp. 9-10; W.I. Singh, pp. 580-81; L.I. Singh, p. 210; Jhalajit Singh, *op. cit.*, p. 138.

85. CK, p. 64.

86. BK, p. 10; Jhalajit Singh, p. 95.

87. CK, p. 122.

88. L.I. Singh, *op.cit.*, p. 211; Jhalajit Singh, p. 206.

89. BK, p. 11.

90. *Op. cit.*, p. 18.
91. *Kirata-Jana-Kriti*, p. 144; see also K.B. Singh, *Himalaya, Man and Nature, III*, 5. October 1979, p. 11.
92. *Op. cit.*, p. 161.
93. Ouoted in Hodson, *op. cit.*, xxi; see also H. Lyall, *Asiatic Studies*, I, p. 113.
94. See also G.P. Singh, "Aryanisation, Brahmanisation and Sanskritization in the Valley of Manipur in North-East India; A Historical Reappraisal," *Journal of Historical Research* (Deptt. of history, Dibrugarh University, Dibrugarh), IX, 1999, p. 32.
95. ERE, VIII, 1964, p. 402.
96. *The Meitheis*, pp. 95 and 97. One of the observations made by Charles Eliot (a noted authority on Hinduism and Buddhism), though of general nature, deserves mention here: "Hinduism is an unusual combination of animism and pantheism, which are commonly regarded as the extremes of...philosophic belief. In India both may be found separately but frequently they are combined in startling juxtaposition. The same person who worships Vishnu as identical with the universe also worships him in the form of a pebble or plant. The average Hindu, who cannot live permanently in the altitudes of pantheistic thought, regards his gods as great natural forces, akin to the mighty rivers which he also worships, irresistible and often beneficent but also capricious and destructive...The bottles of Hinduism

have always proved capable of holding all the wine poured into them."–*Hinduism and Buddhism: An Historical Sketch*, Vol. II, pp. 167-68.

97. "The Religion of Manipur", TFLS, XXIV, 4, 1913, p. 414f.
98. *Op. cit.*, p. 153.
99. B.C. Allen, E.A. Gait, C. G.H. Allen and H.F. Howard, *Gazetteer of Bengal and North-East India* (Delhi, 1979), pp. 39 and 614.
100. ERE, VIII, p. 402.
101. *The Meitheis*, pp. 112 and 116.
102. *Ibid., p. 112.*
103. CK, pp. 66-69, 85-87.
104. *Ibid.*, pp. 140, 142.
105. See CK, pp. 73-74; Hodson, *op.cit.*, p. 116f; N. Khelchandra Singh, "Manipurda Hindu Dharmagi prabhab," SMRHS, Imphal, Dec. 1981 (*supra*).
106. CK, pp. 74-78.
107. For details see N. Khelchandra Singh, *Ariba Manipuri Sahityagi Itihasa*, pp. 39-42.
108. S. K. Chatterji, *Kirata-Jana-Kriti*, p. 48.
109. For details see *Coins of Manipur, Bulletin* No. 1 (MM, Imphal, October, 1980).
110. *Ibid.*, pp. 15-21; Gunindra Singh, *op.cit.*, pp. 66-78.
111. *Coins of Manipur*, Bulletin No. 1 (*Supra*), p. 22.

112. ERM, I, pp. 8-13, 18.
113. CK, pp. 50-60.
114. *Manipur Temple Architecture, Bulletin* No. 3 (MM, Imphal, Aug. 1983), pp. 12-13.
115. *Ibid.*, p.13.
116. *Ibid.*, pp. 36-43.
117. *Sculptures of Manipur, Bulletin* No. 2 (MM, Imphal, Dec. 1982).
118. For details see *Ibid.*
119. *Op. cit.*,pp. 96-97.
120. *Cf* TFLS, XXIV, 4, 1913, pp. 518-23.
121. *Op. cit.*, pp. 17-18.
122. Quoted in Hodson, *op.cit.*, XXI.

INDEX